STATIONS OF THE RISEN CHRIST

EASTER REFLECTIONS

BY FRANK HEELAN

The watermark image of the Risen Christ behind the Reading for each Station was created from a photo taken of the statue of Christ at the Resurrection Cemetery in Piscataway, New Jersey.

The images used for Stations 1, 3, 5, 6, 9 and 11 were taken from the collections of Felix Just, S. J. at http://myweb.lmu.edu/fjust/Dore.htm; those for Stations 2, 4, and 8, from Rolf E. Staerk's web site, Biblical Art on the www; and the rest, from several web sites of Jerome Dominguez, M.D., Ph.D.

Acknowledgement is given to Joan Zayac, for typing the text and Julieta Santos, for editing, formatting and designing the booklet.

Stations of the Risen Christ
is written by Frank Heelan
Copyright 2007, Frank Heelan

Published and Printed by:
Lifevest Publishing
4901 E. Dry Creek Rd., #170
Centennial, CO 80122
www.lifevestpublishing.com

Printed in the United States of America

I.S.B.N. 1-59879-393-4

STATIONS OF THE RISEN CHRIST

First   The Women Find the Empty Tomb

Second   The Women Tell the Disciples

Third   Peter and the Disciple Run to the Tomb

Fourth   Jesus Appears to Mary Magdalene

Fifth   Jesus and the Disciples Walk to Emmaus

Sixth   Jesus Appears to His Disciples

Seventh   Thomas Believes

Eighth   Jesus Appears to the Disciples at Lake Tiberias

Ninth   Jesus Shares a Meal with the Disciples

Tenth   Jesus Commissions Peter "Feed My Sheep"

Eleventh   Jesus Says, "Go, Teach All Peoples"

Twelfth   Jesus Ascends into Heaven

Thirteenth   The Holy Spirit Fills Believers

Fourteenth   Jesus Will Come Again

Introduction

Jesus Christ suffered a humiliating and agonizing death on the cross in expiation for our sins. Christ's followers must accept the suffering and crosses of their lives in union with Christ, our Savior and our Exemplar. For centuries, Christians have devoutly prayed the Stations of the Cross to commemorate the suffering and death of Jesus on the cross and to remind us that we also have a share in Christ's suffering and death through our daily lives.

The disciples of Jesus experienced the reality of Christ's Resurrection from the dead, his many appearances to his disciples culminating in his Ascension into heaven and the sending of the Advocate, the Helper, the Holy Spirit to his disciples. Christians relive these experiences during the Easter season and long for the day beyond this world's inevitable crosses, hardships and death when we will reach the other side and experience Jesus in heaven with our own resurrected bodies.

The "Stations of the Risen Christ" capture fourteen vignettes from the Gospel writings of John, Luke and Matthew that focus on the hope of Jesus' Resurrection, Ascension and the Descent of the Holy Spirit upon the disciples. A brief meditation follows each of the fourteen Scripture readings to motivate readers to pray and acquire a deeper understanding of these divine mysteries.

"Alleluia! Alleluia! Let the Holy Anthem Rise" is recommended as a prefatory hymn for the Stations of the Risen Christ and "Jesus is Risen" by Lasst Uns Erfreuen as the concluding hymn.

Alleluia! Alleluia! Let the Holy Anthem Rise

1. Al - le - lu - ia! Al - le - lu - ia! Let the
3. Al - le - lu - ia! Al - le - lu - ia! Like the
5. Al - le - lu - ia! Al - le - lu - ia! Bless - ed

ho - ly an - them rise, And the choirs of heav - en
sun from out the wave He has ris - en up in
Je - sus, make us rise From the life of this cor -

chant it In the tem - ple of the skies; Let the
tri - umph From the dark - ness of the grave. He's the
rup - tion To the life that nev - er dies. May we

moun - tains skip with glad - ness And the
splen - dor of the na - tions; He's the
share with you your glo - ry When the

joy - ful val - leys ring With ho - san - nas in the
lamp of end - less day; He's the ver - y Lord of
days of time are past, And the dead shall be a -

high - est To our Sav - ior and our King!
glo - ry Who is ris - en up to - day!
wak - ened By the trum - pet's might - y blast!

Text: Edward Caswall, 1814-1878
Tune: HOLY ANTHEM, 8 7 8 7 D; traditional melody; harm. by Jerry R. Brubaker, b.1946

3

THE FIRST STATION

The Women Find the Empty Tomb

V.   *Alleluia! Christ is risen!*
R.   *The Lord is risen indeed, alleluia!*

Very early on Sunday morning the women went to the tomb carrying the spices they had prepared. They found the stone rolled away from the entrance to the tomb so they went in, but they did not find the body of the Lord Jesus. They stood there puzzled about this when suddenly two men in bright shining clothes stood by them. Full of fear, the women bowed down to the ground as the men said to them, "Why are you looking among the dead for one who is alive? He is not here; he has been raised. Remember what he said to you while he was in Galilee: 'The Son of Man must be handed over to sinful men to be crucified, and three days later rise to life."

Luke 24:1-7

MEDITATION

Let us Pray:

O Jesus, the women were fearful at finding that the tomb was empty and your body had vanished, but imagine the exuberant joy the women felt when the two angels informed them that you were raised from the dead. Enhance our faith, O Jesus, to believe firmly that you conquered death by rising from the dead.

THE SECOND STATION

The Women Tell the Disciples

V. *Alleluia! Christ is risen!*
R. *The Lord is risen indeed, alleluia!*

Then the women remembered his words, returned from the tomb, and told all these things to the eleven disciples and all the rest. The women were Mary Magdalene, Joanna, and Mary, the mother of James. They and the other women with them told these things to the apostles. But the apostles thought that what the women said was nonsense, and they did not believe them.

Luke 24:8-11

MEDITATION

V. *The Lord be with you.*
R. *And also with you.*

Let us Pray:

O Jesus, how could the apostles not believe the women who told them that the tomb was empty and you had risen from the dead? Give us the grace to understand and believe that you, Jesus Christ, were crucified for our sins and rose from the dead three days later.

THE THIRD STATION

Peter and the Disciple Run to the Tomb

V.   *Alleluia! Christ is risen!*
R.   *The Lord is risen indeed, alleluia!*

Then Peter and the other disciple went to the tomb. The two of them were running, but the other disciple ran faster than Peter and reached the tomb first. He bent over and saw the linen cloths but he did not go in. Behind him came Simon Peter and he went straight into the tomb. He saw the linen cloths lying there and the cloth that had been around Jesus' head. It was not lying with the linen cloths but was rolled up by itself. Then the other disciple, who had reached the tomb first, also went in. He saw and believed.

John 20:3-8

MEDITATION

Let us Pray:

O Jesus, help us to run faster than Peter in reaching the empty tomb and in finding only linen cloths where you had been buried. Wrap our heads in the linen cloths that circumscribed the bloody, thorny crown around your head. Give us the belief of the "other" disciple who first reached the tomb and the courage of Peter who unhesitatingly entered into the tomb.

THE FOURTH STATION

Jesus Appears to Mary Magdalene

V. *Alleluia! Christ is risen!*
R. *The Lord is risen indeed, alleluia!*

Then Mary Magdalene turned around and saw Jesus standing there; but she did not know it was Jesus. "Woman, why are you crying?" Jesus asked her. "Who is it that you are looking for?"

She thought he was the gardener, so she said to him, "If you took him away, sir, tell me where you have put him, and I will go and get him." Jesus said to her, "Mary!"

She turned toward him and said in Hebrew, "Rabboni!" which means "Teacher."

"Do not hold on to me," Jesus told her, "because I have not yet gone back up to the Father. But go to my brothers and tell them that I am returning to Him who is my Father and their Father, my God and their God."

John 20:11-17

MEDITATION

*V.	The Lord be with you.*
*R.	And also with you.*

Let us Pray:

O Jesus, how is it that Mary Magdalene, who knew you so well throughout your three years of ministry and was present at your crucifixion, didn't recognize you and thought you were the gardener? Only when you called Mary Magdalene by her name did she recognize you as "Teacher." Let us know that you are our Teacher, Jesus, who calls us by name and give us the grace to follow your commandments to reach eternal life.

THE FIFTH STATION

Jesus and the Disciples Walk to Emmaus

V.   *Alleluia! Christ is risen!*
R.   *The Lord is risen indeed, alleluia!*

Jesus said to the two disciples, "How foolish you are, and how slow to believe everything the prophets said! Was it not necessary for the Messiah to suffer these things and then to enter this glory?"   And Jesus explained to them what was said about himself in all the Scriptures, beginning with the books of Moses and the writings of all the prophets.

As they came near the village to which they were going, Jesus acted as if he were going further; but they held him back saying, "Stay with us; the day is almost over and it is getting dark." So he went in to stay with them. He sat down to eat with them, took the bread, and said the blessing; then he broke the bread and gave it to them. Then their eyes were opened and they recognized him, but he disappeared from their sight. They said to each other, "Wasn't it like a fire burning in us when he talked to us on the road and explained the Scriptures to us?"

Luke 24:25-32

MEDITATION

V.   *The Lord be with you.*
R.   *And also with you.*

Let us Pray:

O Jesus, may you walk with us on the path of life and guide our footsteps in seeking your will. Stay with us and illuminate our minds to comprehend you, Jesus, as the fulfillment of the Scriptures. May we continue to know you in the blessing, breaking and eating of your flesh in the Holy Eucharist.

THE SIXTH STATION

Jesus Appears to His Disciples

V.   *Alleluia! Christ is risen!*
R.   *The Lord is risen indeed, alleluia!*

It was late that Sunday evening, and the disciples were gathered together behind locked doors because they were afraid of the Jewish authorities. Then Jesus came and stood among them. "Peace be with you," he said. After saying this, he showed them his hands and his side. The disciples were filled with joy at seeing the Lord. Jesus said to them again, "Peace be with you. As the Father sent me, so I send you." Then he breathed on them and said, "Receive the Holy Spirit. If you forgive people's sins, they are forgiven; if you do not forgive them, they are not forgiven."

John 20:19-23

MEDITATION

V.   *The Lord be with you.*
R.   *And also with you.*

Let us Pray:

O Jesus, the disciples were trembling in fear behind locked doors when you came and brought "peace" to them. Jesus, breathe your Spirit upon us so that we may cast out fear, be filled with genuine joy and realize how we are being sent by you to be a witness and to convey that joy to others.

THE SEVENTH STATION

Thomas Believes

V.   *Alleluia! Christ is risen!*
R.   *The Lord is risen indeed, alleluia!*

One of the twelve disciples, Thomas, called the Twin, was not with them when Jesus came. So, the other disciples told him, "We have seen the Lord."

Thomas said to them, "Unless I see the scars of the nails in his hands and put my finger on those scars and my hand in his side, I will not believe."

A week later the disciples were together again indoors, and Thomas was with them. The doors were locked, but Jesus came and stood among them and said, "Peace be with you." Then he said to Thomas, "Put your finger here, and look at my hands; then reach out your hand and put it in my side. Stop your doubting and believe!"

Thomas answered him, "My Lord and my God!" Jesus said to him, "Do you believe because you see me? How happy are those who believe without seeing me!"

John 20:24-29

MEDITATION

Let us Pray:

O Jesus, Thomas refused to believe in your resurrected body and only believed after he placed his fingers on your scarred hands and side. Dispel any doubts we may have about the truths of your crucifixion and resurrection so that our faith may be so strengthened that we may burst out with Thomas exclaiming, "My Lord and my God!"

THE EIGHTH STATION

Jesus Appears to the Disciples at Lake Tiberias

After this, Jesus appeared once more to his disciples at Lake Tiberias. This is how it happened. Simon Peter, Thomas, Nathaniel, the sons of Zebedee, and two other disciples of Jesus were all together. Simon Peter said to the others, "I am going fishing."

"We will come with you," they told him. So they went out in a boat, but all that night they did not catch a thing. As the sun was rising Jesus stood at the water's edge, but the disciples did not know that it was Jesus. Then he asked them, "Young men, haven't you caught anything?"

"Not a thing," they answered.

He said to them, "Throw your net out on the right side of the boat and you will catch some." So they threw the net out and could not pull it in, because they had caught so many fish.

The disciple whom Jesus loved said to Peter, "It is the Lord!"

John 21:1-7

18

MEDITATION

V.   *The Lord be with you.*
R.   *And also with you.*

Let us Pray:

O Jesus, once again the disciples didn't know you until you showed your power over nature. You appeared as the sun was rising and dispelled the darkness of their anxieties and filled their nets with fish. John was the first to realize "It is the Lord!" and the disciples would soon know that they would be fishing for other followers of Christ. Jesus, let us recognize you in other people and be a witness to your saving power.

THE NINTH STATION

Jesus Shares a Meal with the Disciples

V.   *Alleluia! Christ is risen!*
R.   *The Lord is risen indeed, alleluia!*

When they stepped ashore, they saw a charcoal fire there with fish on it and some bread. Then Jesus said, "Bring some of the fish you have just caught."

Simon Peter went aboard and dragged out the net full of big fish, a hundred and fifty three in all; even though there were so many, still the net did not tear. Jesus said to them, "Come and eat." None of the disciples dared ask him, "Who are you?" because they knew it was the Lord. So Jesus went over, took the bread, and gave it to them; he did the same with the fish.

John 21:9-13

MEDITATION

V.   *The Lord be with you.*
R.   *And also with you.*

Let us Pray:

O Jesus, the disciples must have felt bizarre sharing a meal of fish and bread with you after you suffered, died and were raised from the dead. Give us hope that when our earthly bodies rise from the dead and we have a new heavenly body, we may be nourished by sharing a meal with you on the seashore.

THE TENTH STATION

Jesus Commissions Peter
"Feed My Sheep"

V.   *Alleluia! Christ is risen!*
R.   *The Lord is risen indeed, alleluia!*

When they had finished breakfast, Jesus said to Simon Peter, "Simon, son of John, do you love me more than these?" Simon Peter answered him, "Yes, Lord you know that I love you." Jesus said to him, "Feed my lambs." He then said to Simon Peter a second time, "Simon, son of John, do you love me?" Simon Peter answered him, "Yes, Lord you know that I love you." Jesus said to him, "Tend my sheep." Jesus said to him a third time, "Simon, son of John, do you love me?" Peter was distressed that Jesus had said to him a third time, "Do you love me?" and he said to him, "Lord you know everything; you know that I love you." Jesus said to him, "Feed my sheep."

John 21:15-17

MEDITATION

V.   *The Lord be with you.*
R.   *And also with you.*

Let us Pray:

O Jesus, three times you challenged Peter with the question, "Do you love me?" and in contrast to his threefold denial before your crucifixion, Peter vigorously insisted on his love for you. Jesus, you then enjoined Peter three times to "Feed my sheep!" Overwhelm us with your tremendous love, Lord, and give us the grace to bring your love to others.

THE ELEVENTH STATION

Jesus Says, "Go, Teach All Peoples"

V.   *Alleluia! Christ is risen!*
R.   *The Lord is risen indeed, alleluia!*

The eleven disciples went to the hill in Galilee where Jesus had told them to go. When they saw him, they worshiped him, even though some of them doubted. Jesus drew near and said to them, "I have been given all authority in heaven and on earth. Go, then, to all peoples everywhere and make them my disciples: baptize them in the name of the Father, the Son, and the Holy Spirit and teach them to obey everything I have commanded you. And I will be with you always to the end of time."

Matthew 28:16-20

MEDITATION

V.   The Lord be with you.
R.   And also with you.

Let us Pray:

O Jesus, you have commissioned us to go to all peoples and make them your disciples, baptizing them and teaching them to obey your commandments. Jesus, let us boldly proclaim your word to all peoples, with your assurance that you will be with us to the end of time.

THE TWELFTH STATION

Jesus Ascends into Heaven

V.   *Alleluia! Christ is risen!*
R.   *The Lord is risen indeed, alleluia!*

Then Jesus opened their minds to understand the Scriptures and said to them, "This is what is written: 'The Messiah must suffer and rise from death three days later, and in his name the message about repentance and the forgiveness of sins must be preached to all nations, beginning in Jerusalem. You are witnesses of these things. And I myself will send upon you what my Father has promised.' But you must wait in the city until the power from above comes down upon you."

    Then he led them out of the city as far as Bethany, where he raised his hands and blessed them. As he was blessing them, he departed from them and was taken up into heaven. They worshiped him and went back to Jerusalem, filled with great joy and spent all their time in the Temple giving thanks to God.

Luke 24:45-53

MEDITATION

V.   The Lord be with you.
R.   And also with you.

Let us Pray:

O Jesus, open our minds to understand the Scriptures and to be a witness to your wonderful message of repentance and forgiveness of our sins. May we also worship you and be suffused with awesome wonder at your ascending into heaven after your many appearances to your disciples.

THE THIRTEENTH STATION

The Holy Spirit Fills Believers

V.   *Alleluia! Christ is risen!*
R.   *The Lord is risen indeed, alleluia!*

When the day of Pentecost came, all the believers were gathered together in one place. Suddenly there was a noise from the sky which sounded like strong wind blowing, and it filled the whole house where they were sitting. Then, they saw what looked like tongues of fire which spread out and touched each person there. They were all filled with the Holy Spirit and began to talk in other languages, as the Spirit enabled them to speak.

Acts of the Apostles 2:1-4

MEDITATION

V.   The Lord be with you.
R.   And also with you.

Let us Pray:

O Jesus, true to your promise, the Holy Spirit descended on
the believers in the form of the tongues of fire that enveloped
everyone. As the disciples were filled with the Holy Spirit
and began to talk in other languages, let us pray that the
Spirit will fill our hearts so that we will bear the good news of
Jesus Christ to other people.

THE FOURTEENTH STATION

Jesus Will Come Again

V. *Alleluia! Christ is risen!*
R. *The Lord is risen indeed, alleluia!*

There will be strange things happening to the sun, the moon and the stars. On earth whole countries will be in despair, afraid of the roar of the sea and the raging tides. People will faint from fear as they wait for what is coming over the whole earth, for the powers in space will be driven from their courses. Then the Son of Man will appear, coming in a cloud with great power and glory. When these things begin to happen, stand up and raise your heads, because your salvation is near.

Luke 21:25-28

MEDITATION

V.   *The Lord be with you.*
R.   *And also with you.*

Let us Pray:

O Jesus, we anxiously await your second coming when you will come in a cloud with great power and glory. With the certain knowledge that you are with us personally in the Eucharist or whenever two or three gather in your name, we raise up our heads to heaven, knowing full well that our salvation is at hand.

We eagerly anticipate that day when our bodies will be raised from the dead and we will see your resurrected body, Jesus, in a heaven that "eye has not seen, nor ear heard, nor has it entered into the minds of humans what God has prepared for those who love him."

JESUS IS RISEN

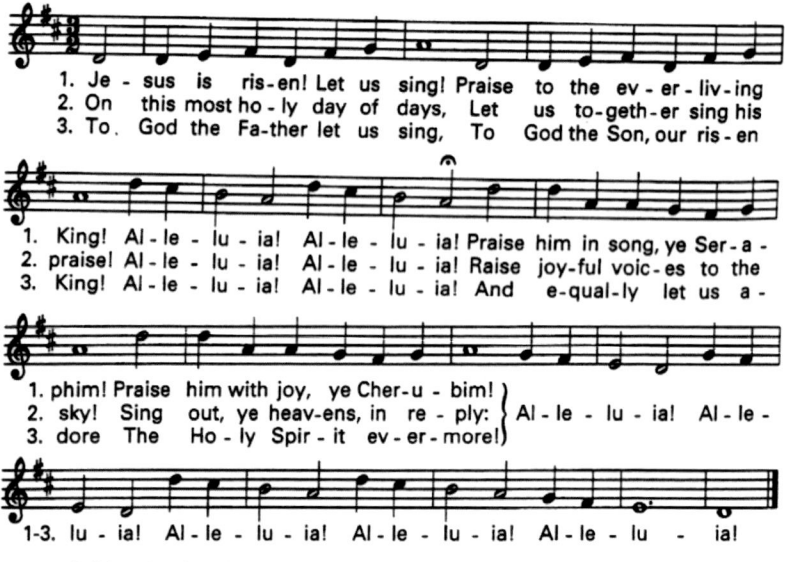

1. Je - sus is ris-en! Let us sing! Praise to the ev - er - liv-ing
2. On this most ho - ly day of days, Let us to-geth-er sing his
3. To. God the Fa-ther let us sing, To God the Son, our ris - en

1. King! Al-le - lu - ia! Al-le - lu - ia! Praise him in song, ye Ser - a -
2. praise! Al-le - lu - ia! Al-le - lu - ia! Raise joy-ful voic-es to the
3. King! Al-le - lu - ia! Al-le - lu - ia! And e-qual-ly let us a -

1. phim! Praise him with joy, ye Cher-u - bim!
2. sky! Sing out, ye heav-ens, in re - ply: } Al - le - lu - ia! Al - le -
3. dore The Ho - ly Spir - it ev - er - more!

1-3. lu - ia! Al-le - lu - ia! Al-le - lu - ia! Al-le - lu - ia!

Text: LM with alleluias; Compilers, 1978.
Music: LASST UNS ERFREUEN; *Auserlesene Catholische Geistliche Kirchengesänge*, Cologne, 1623.

To Order Copies of

Stations
of the Risen Christ
Easter Reflections

by Frank Heelan

I.S.B.N. 1-59879-393-4

Order Online at:
www.authorstobelievein.com

By Phone Toll Free at:
1-877-843-1007